8 INNOVATIONS TO LEADING
MILLENNIALS

How Millennials can grow your church and change the world.

Published by The Thrive Co
www.thethrivecogroup.com

CONTENTS

FOREWARD

Millennials. There could not be a more important and vital group of people to love and support than this generation. I'm sad to say they have been trashed by endless articles and books over the last few years. But the reality is, we are the fathers of this generation. So, if there is a great disaster going on, it's ours to own!

My experience, however, is not one of disaster or problems. I personally think the Millennials are the best to work with. I see greatness in this generation. They have heart, tons of loyalty, compassion, love for justice and a huge disgust for big ego leaders and money wasting organizations! I love their raw honesty, deep authenticity and their hunger to learn. This is their time and I want to be a part of it - finally a great book on the Millennials!

Dr Frank Damazio

Leadership consultant & author of "The Making of a Leader".

ABOUT THE AUTHOR

GRADCERTMGT (QLD.UT), GRADCERTBUSADMIN (DEAKIN), MBA (DEAKIN)

Benjamin is a pastor, author, and life strategist. His 'Life Minute' radio program brings 60 seconds of life skills to more than one million listeners on a daily basis.

Benjamin is married to his high school sweetheart, Cindi, and in their early twenties they moved to the City of Roses—Portland, Oregon—where they worked at City Bible Church for Dr. Frank Damazio. In 2009, they returned with their family to Brisbane to pioneer Lifeplace Church.

Lifeplace Church is now a thriving multi-campus organization serving a diverse range of people.

This insight on Millennials' faith is part of Benjamin's desire to help churches create Generationally Intelligent communities. He advocates that 'New isn't on the way. It's here.'

Benjamin and Cindi currently live in the Gold Coast Hinterland with their three sons, Houston, BJ, and Jameson, and two dogs, Romeo and Juliet.

For more resources please go to:

www.benjaminwindle.com

www.thethrivecogroup.com

www.millennialswhitepaper.com

A

THE NEW WORLD

I am still trying to understand who I am. Born in 1982, I sit on the boundary between Generation X and the Millennials. While I don't completely fit in either generation, my age gives me a unique insight into both.

My childhood involved riding my Huffy BMX bike unsupervised through the leafy Western suburbs of Brisbane, where for 20 cents I could play arcade video games at the local fish and chip shop. My only rule—come home when the sun sets. Atari. Hyper-color t-shirts. The Wonder Years. The 80s was a cool decade to grow up in!

I am also an early settler of the digital era. I'm not a true native, but I was young enough when the digital revolution hit to catch the first wave and adopt technology early. I was streaming movies before Blockbuster went bankrupt. I was blogging at 18. I traveled the world in my early twenties, seeking experiences over structure. I rejected the hierarchical church structures I was raised in, and went in search of more fluid, relational models. I embraced technology instinctively as a norm in almost every area of my life.

I have experienced life in both analog and digital. My childhood and early teens were not just another era; they were another way of living that has long passed. True Millennials and Generation Z have only ever known a digital world. Their worldview starts at a very different place than all other generations.

The sound of dial-up Internet is still familiar to me. I can remember searching for the VHS tape behind the cover in Blockbuster video stores, and I even carried a Walkman on the way to school to play cassette tapes. I grew up in an analog environment, but during my teenage years, I also experienced the genesis of the digital age.

True Millennials and Generation Z have only ever known a digital world. Their worldview starts at a very different place than all other generations.
BENJAMIN WINDLE

I speak from the paradigm of living in both worlds.

Gen Y, also known as Millennials because they came of age as they crossed from the 20th to 21st centuries, witnessed the advent of new technologies. Computers became personal, and the Internet became a reality. Gen Z, on the other hand, has only ever known social media, Uber, cellular devices, wearable technology, and the like.

As a pastor, I can straddle the cultural mindset of multiple eras, especially Generations Y and Z. The true Gen Y, and especially Gen Z, are digital natives in today's world, whereas the rest of us are digital immigrants.

To be candid, I almost left the church for good. It had nothing to do with God, and nothing to do with the people—it had everything to do with culture and methodology. I was reacting to something I couldn't articulate at the time: a set of unseen cultural expressions that iceberged into something large and obstructive beneath the water. Culturally, the hull had collided, and water was gushing in. I wanted to jump ship. I was raised in the church. My father was a pastor.

At the age of 17, I came to a fork in the road. Was this only the religion of my parents, or was I going to stay? Ultimately, I made a crucial decision to be a church builder instead of a church critic. I didn't leave the church. I stayed because the local church is central to the Christian faith in the New Testament. I stayed because if you want to change something, you have to first love it and embrace it. I stayed because, despite some imperfections, my life was changed through the local church.

So, at 17, I graduated high school, started a small group in my local church, and made a touchstone commitment in my heart to Jesus that has guided my path for 20 years: I will stay and be a part of building what you are building—the church. From that point on, my passion has been the local church.

It doesn't surprise me when I read almost universal statistics of Millennials abandoning church. Church, unlike many other industries, has not had its prevailing model disrupted by generational change or technology to the extent that it has been forced to undergo a complete rebuild. Think Kodak film vs. digital cameras. Airbnb vs. the hotel industry. Uber vs. taxis. If church history teaches us anything about ourselves, it is this: we (the church) have a remarkable ability to insulate against mega-changes in society and maintain our status quo.

This protectionist approach, often wrapped in theological dogmas and cliché statements like "Truth never changes," means we stay… the… same. And the world changes. Let me say emphatically, I am an orthodox, Bible-believing follower of Jesus. All the core tenants of theology that conservative Christians have believed for many generations—yep, I believe them. With that out of the way, I can push my point that maintaining a timeless biblical theology does not absolve us of the necessity of reinventing our methodologies to cater to a new world. In fact, a good doctrinal conversation could be had around God as a creator, innovator, and *surpriser*—often doing things in new and unexpected ways!

The prevailing model of church will be disrupted to a much greater degree than what we are presently seeing. A protectionist mindset will neither delay nor prevent the loss of Millennials from the church. This is the most exciting time to be alive. And it is time to unleash a new wave of innovation, progress, and dare I say, experimentation with our ministry models. We have to try new things.

But before we try to DO new things, we have to BE something new. New programs, new events, new marketing—Millennials have seen it all, and they can spot it a mile away. We need something deeper, something that dwells less in programs and more in philosophy.

> **The prevailing model of church will be disrupted to a much greater degree than what we are presently seeing. A protectionist mindset will neither delay nor prevent the loss of Millennials from the church.**
>
> **BENJAMIN WINDLE**

Surface level changes that don't dive deep into why we do what we do, and that don't address the core generational issues, will only band-aid the issue. It is these same surface level changes that I see many churches making (young people want cooler services, better lights and sound, modern music, better social media) that makes me think we can't just change a few stylistic elements while keeping the same underlying model of how we think as leaders and churches.

It is Blockbuster in the early 2000s, making a half-hearted attempt at hedging off Netflix by offering downloadable movies, but still pushing those customers to their physical stores. Why? Their executives believed people would still come to stores to buy popcorn and confectionary. So, yes, they changed and added an online option. But it was a thinly veiled attempt to appear to be relevant to a changing world, without changing their core structure and model. The executives did not change their *mindset* until it was too late. They couldn't compete against companies like Netflix, who not only offered more intuitive online options, but philosophically speaking were, culturally, a different species of organization altogether.

IT IS A GENERATION THAT CLEARLY CARRIES THE FINGERPRINT OF GOD

BENJAMIN WINDLE

The few mega-successful Millennial churches do not make up for what is an overwhelming generational trend away from the church.

Experimentation should be embraced. Trying different things should be celebrated. In fact, experimentation is an expression of humility—inherent in an experiment is the idea that we don't know for sure—and it is the humility that people are drawn to, even if the experiment fails.

We need to study and reach Millennials like a mission field. Change or decline. Change or die.

I write this systematic analysis and set of solutions to pastoring Millennials not just as a practitioner and pastor, but as one of them. I write as a Millennial.

Yes, I am saying we must first understand before being understood.

Yes, I believe we can reach Millennials and Gen Z at an unprecedented rate, and the opportunity is great.

Yes, I am advocating new thinking for a new world.

Yes, I believe Jesus is building His church, and that the greatest days are yet to come!

Churches age naturally. It takes intentionality, social design, and foresight for leaders to keep reaching each successive generation.

The few mega-successful Millennial churches do not make up for what is an overwhelming generational trend away from the church.
BENJAMIN WINDLE

One generation passes away, and another generation comes; But the earth abides forever.

Ecclesiastes 1:4 (NKJV)

Generations are passing away. Will your church pass away with them?

Our present culture is like a shifting shadow in the afternoon sun of culture. Will the church be left behind, or will we understand "the times and seasons" and harness the endless opportunities this new generation brings?

Millennials are optimists, talented, creative, and collaborators. They are also driven by a thirst for significance. They are relational, and have an inbuilt desire for authenticity. They will serve when challenged, and have ideas that are already revolutionizing the world. In fact, when you look at these characteristics another way, it reveals Millennials carry the traits of exceptional leadership. Don't buy into the negativity against Millennials; they are remarkable. They are world-changers and hard workers.

In other words, this is a generation to love and be inspired by. It is a generation that clearly carries the fingerprint of God. And as church leaders, we will pivot. We will adjust. God will give us creative ideas to reach a new generation like He always has. New models will arise. Your most exciting and rewarding days may be ahead of you as you see this generation shine and innovate.

My thesis is clear and bold: Millennials can grow your church and change the world.

Don't buy into the negativity against Millennials; they are remarkable. They are world-changers and hard workers.
BENJAMIN WINDLE

SAY HELLO TO MILLENNIALS AND GEN Z

It's a different world.

The time-honored structures, languages, facilities, and approaches from the past won't work today. A new generation is here, and they think, relate, and live differently than any other generation before them. I am optimistic about this new generation. They are hopeful, educated, and believe they can change the world.

Mega-trends and broad patterns have created a new era. It's already arrived, and it is fundamentally changing society.

People now live thirty years longer than they once did. In 1900, the average life span was forty-eight; today, it's seventy-eight. But as people live longer—for which we're all grateful—it presents new challenges that previous eras didn't face. In previous eras, there were only three generations.

But today, for the first time in history, we have five generations in our families, churches, and communities. Five. That's a huge change, and it causes quite a shake-up because every generation is pushing to be heard and understood…

This is the first time we have five generations alive at the same time, and we don't have the generational intelligence to handle it yet.

Generational IQ: Christianity Isn't Dying, Millennials Aren't the Problem, and the Future is Bright

I am optimistic about this new generation. They are hopeful, educated, and believe they can change the world.
BENJAMIN WINDLE

Defining Gen Y: The Millennials

"Over time a society mutates, and at a certain point in that development we draw a hazy line to mark a generation."

Kids These Days: Human Capital and the Making of Millennials

Generations are now typically defined in 15-year time brackets. Our society is currently made up of five generations:

Builders—Traditionalists, and the Silent Generation (born pre-1945)

Baby Boomers (born 1946-1964)

Generation X (born 1965-1979)

Generation Y—The Millennials (born 1980-2001)

Generation Z—The Post-Millennials (born 2001 onwards)

Which Generation You're in Based on Your Birth Year

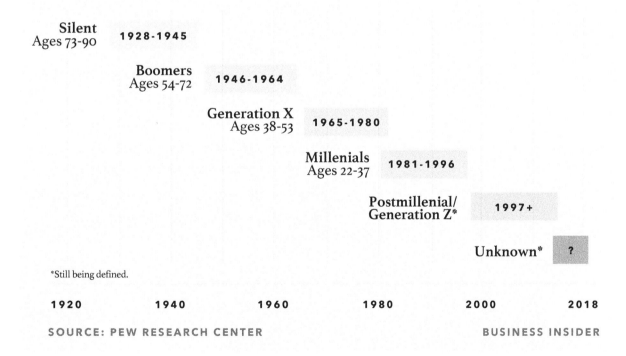

Silent
Ages 73-90   1928-1945

Boomers
Ages 54-72   1946-1964

Generation X
Ages 38-53   1965-1980

Millenials
Ages 22-37   1981-1996

Postmillenial/
Generation Z*   1997+

Unknown*   ?

*Still being defined.

1920   1940   1960   1980   2000   2018

SOURCE: PEW RESEARCH CENTER   BUSINESS INSIDER

Increased life expectancy has led to multiple generations living simultaneously, and it presents unique and unprecedented challenges to relate to people that where raised in such vastly different moments of human history. While we may assume that technology or world events are shaping the landscape of culture, it is hard to get around this fact that there are more generations alive at the same time than any other point in history.

Each of these generations was raised in vastly different worlds.

The Silent Generation sacrificed their needs and those of their families. Many of them lived through the Great Depression and witnessed World War II. Their children, the Baby Boomers, embraced consumerism and excess. Boomer millionaire Malcomb Forbes coined the slogan, "He who dies with the most toys, wins."

Having seen the excess material goods collected by their parents, Gen X and the Millennials are more prone to focus on the quality of their lives than the quantity of their collections. They can view ownership as less important than lifestyle.

These vast differences can cause generations to misunderstand each other.

Increased life expectancy has led to multiple generations living simultaneously, and it presents unique and unprecedented challenges to relate to people that where raised in such vastly different moments of human history.
BENJAMIN WINDLE

So, it is easy to see why we need the ability to relate to and build rapport with more generations. Generational literacy and intelligence are fundamental to communicating with each generation to understand its needs, especially those of the Millennials.

Put simply, the ability to understand and relate to multiple generations at one time is more crucial than ever before.

So, why the emphasis on reaching Millennials?

> "To handle this new world, we need generational intelligence. The reason we struggle with other generations is not that they are 'the problem.' The reason we struggle with other generations is that we don't understand them."
>
> Generational Iq: Christianity Isn't Dying, Millennials Aren't the Problem, and the Future is Bright

We must pay attention to those who make up the Millennial generation by getting to know them and discovering the answers to questions like these:

How do they live?

How did they get here?

Where will their paths take them?

What does their faith look like?

Why do they not attend church as much as the generations who have gone before?

The common misconception about Millennials is that they are entitled basement-dwellers who are content to let their best years slip past them.

Nothing could be further from the truth.

With the advent of the 21st century, we are facing a mega-shift in culture, church attendance, and religious beliefs. Everything is changing at a dizzying rate. In the midst of this metamorphosis, we have a generation that will change the way entire industries operate. Millennials are already redefining the world in which they want to live.

In the coming years, Millennials will soon make up the vast majority of the global workforce. . By 2030, Millennials will represent 75% of the global workforce. Will they represent 75% of your church?

Millennials and their life experiences represent the most fundamental change in the story of multiple generations to date. They herald a new era of believers and doers. To understand and effectively prepare Millennials for their roles, we must practice generational intelligence as we influence and inspire the generation with the power to change the world.

BY 2030, MILLENNIALS WILL REPRESENT 75% OF THE GLOBAL WORKFORCE. WILL THEY REPRESENT 75% OF YOUR CHURCH?

BENJAMIN WINDLE

GENERATIONAL PATTERNS

As Millennials take their place in leadership roles, their innovations are challenging the prevailing models in almost every industry. Some of these challenges are obvious and driven by technology. Others are subtler, and they have a lot more to do with human behavior and culture.

Consider these examples from the business world:

Amazon

The online retail behemoth Amazon almost single-handedly cannibalized brick and mortar bookstores. Amazon led a change in technology and development that was not embraced by the bookstore organizations who maintained a protectionist paper-only mentality. Consumers download hundreds of millions of ebooks annually. Not only are bookstores now few and far between, but entirely paper-free workplaces are now increasingly becoming a reality.

Airbnb and Uber

Two radical concepts in two different spaces have again almost single-handedly upturned the long-established status quo in their industries. Airbnb and Uber have created a sense of a new normal, and the accommodations and taxi-service industries will never be the same. Individualist, grass-roots approaches, backed by new technology and embraced by millions, have rapidly and radically changed many years of established models and traditions.

Kodak

Despite creating the household slogan "a Kodak moment," and once holding the dominant position in photographic film worldwide, Kodak's slowness in transitioning to digital photography led to bankruptcy and the company nearly disappeared.

Churches face the challenge to change with the times, too. It's less a church issue and more a subtle, profound cultural shift among Millennials that is causing the change.

These are a few of the trends today:

Secularization

In secularization, religion and the religious values associated with it disappear from culture and are replaced with government ideals and other secular institutions. Religion loses its influence over people as they embrace non-religious movements.

> **Technology has permeated every area of our lives and become central to how we live, work, and socialize.**
> BENJAMIN WINDLE

Gender revolution

Gender revolution broadly refers to the sweeping changes that are occurring in the gender system where the traditional, binary categories of "male" and "female" are deemed insufficient or invalid. Genders are becoming fluid, even optional.

Privatization

Privatization occurs when the government awards its ownership and control of a business or property to an individual or individuals.

Pluralization

Pluralization, or a plural society, is one where the idea of truth is not absolute. There are many options.

Technology revolution

From the last part of the 20th century to the present, technology has permeated every area of our lives and become central to how we live, work, and socialize. We have moved from an analog world of isolation to a digital one that is connected globally.

Hyper-individualism

Hyper-individualism occurs when an individual need is elevated above the needs of the collective society. It's an "all about me" attitude that takes into account little consideration of others.

Consumerism

Consumerism is the pursuit of money and things that is never satisfied.

These seven trends affect every aspect of modern life. When we start to drill down and look more closely at the influence of these trends, we can begin to understand how and why the local church is also being impacted, and why we need to take notice as well as action.

MILLENNIALS AND THE CHURCH

The shift created by Millennials is not about creating change for the sake of change.

Not only is Christianity (in the broader sense) on the decline, but it is perceived as irrelevant. Millennials have little if any connection to traditional religion and the church. For many, attending church is a peripheral activity unrelated to their daily lives.

Let's look at some recent news articles and studies. The numbers are astonishing.

Why Millennials are really leaving religion (it's not just politics, folks)

"The number of Americans ages 18-29 who have no religious affiliation has nearly quadrupled in the last 30 years." [i]

The Decline of Religious Affiliation Among Young Adults

"Today, nearly four in ten (39%) young adults (ages 18-29) are religiously unaffiliated—three times the unaffiliated rate (13%) among seniors (ages 65 and older). While previous generations were also more likely to be religiously unaffiliated in their twenties, young adults today are nearly four times as likely as young adults a generation ago to identify as religiously unaffiliated." [ii]

Five Reasons Millennials Are Leaving the Church

"Tragically, many churches seem to repel them, despite their best efforts. According to Barna Group, 6 in 10 Millennials who grew up in church have dropped out at some point." [iii]

59 Percent of Millennials Raised in a Church Have Dropped Out—And They're Trying to Tell Us Why

"35 percent of Millennials have an anti-church stance, believing the church does more harm than good." [iv]

Millennials leaving church in droves, CNN study finds

"In the meantime, almost every major branch of Christianity in the United States has lost a significant number of members, Pew found, mainly because Millennials are leaving the fold. More than one-third of Millennials now say they are unaffiliated with any faith, up 10 percentage points since 2007. The alacrity of their exodus surprises even seasoned experts." [v]

An Epidemic? Why Millennials Are Abandoning the Church

"CBN News recently reported on the growth of the "None" movement. "Nones" are people identifying themselves as having no religious affiliation. Many believe there is a God but have lost the desire to be affiliated with a religion." [vi]

If you zoom in on the younger generations, you'll find that their affinity towards attending church is in rapid freefall. It is no longer viable to say of your church, "Well, we have timeless principles..." because soon enough you'll look around and say "...and we have no one under 40."

The numbers paint an important picture. Churches that are successful with Millennials exist. But they are holes in the shoebox letting in rays of light. We can be encouraged by them and learn from them. But on the broader landscape of generational trends, they are anomalies and do not constitute a pattern. And, my crucial point is, these few success stories can be so compelling that they can almost mask the degree of severity of the trend. Please note, it is the big trend that matters. Looking coldly in the face of the numbers is not fatalism or lack of faith—it is reality. Furthermore, when we understand the numbers, it gives rise to new answers and solutions.

> **It is no longer viable to say of your church, "Well, we have timeless principles..." because soon enough you'll look around and say "...and we have no-one under 40".**
>
> **BENJAMIN WINDLE**

Key analogy: The Western-world church is a train

Church in the Western world is like a train with many carriages.

Some churches are growing with young people, creating community and purpose, and filling up with worshippers. Focusing exclusively on these vibrant churches, however, is like looking at just some of the train's carriages, while ignoring the others.

In those energy-filled carriages, the people are cool: you'll find parties, life, and health. The social media photos prove it. We can say, 'Hey, look at the party going on here, look at the success!'

If we only looked in those carriages, we would come to the conclusion that the overall train journey is a fabulous success. But, upon closer inspection, something else has happened.

Three stations earlier, many people got off. The journey didn't interest them. Some train carriages are empty, or they're in total disrepair. The train has slowed down. Its overall direction has veered off course.

The point is that while we see some churches thriving and growing—alive on social media and at global conferences—church in the Western world is on the overall decline with Millennials.

It's tempting to zoom in exclusively on the success of a few carriages. But we have to look at the overall train. We cannot measure the success of the journey unless we take every carriage and the people in them into consideration.

There are a number of further generational trends or concepts that fundamentally impact our specific context of the church today.

Post-Christian world

Millennials are, predominantly, biblically illiterate. They grew up in an increasingly anti-Christian worldview that saw little justification for religious tenets and principles. Bible stories are no longer common knowledge, and parables are largely unknown. Biblical metaphors, such as the burning bush or having faith like a mustard seed, are lost on many Millennials. Even the most basic understanding of Jesus as a historical figure, let alone God, has been rapidly falling out of Western-world common general knowledge.

Post-church era

Millennials outside the church don't understand the value and conviction of the local church, nor its purpose in the community. They often don't understand the role of the pastor. Most Millennials start with an anti-church view of the world.

"The shocking reality for us is that only 13 percent of the Millennials considered any type of spirituality to be important in their lives."

Thom S. Rainer, The Millennials: Connecting To America's Largest Generation

Some raised in the Pentecostal/ charismatic stream have watched the previous generations of their parents and grandparents, causing them to ask - does this even work? Or are they dynamic at church but dysfunctional at life?
BENJAMIN WINDLE

Conservative and Pentecostal reactions

Not all Millennials grew up outside the church. Millennials who have been raised in the church, like myself, face some unique dynamics.

Church-attending Millennials saw their parents falling over and being "slain in the spirit" on a Sunday and getting divorced on a Monday. Some raised in the Pentecostal/charismatic stream have watched the previous generations of their parents and grandparents, causing them to ask – does this even work? Or are they dynamic at church but dysfunctional at life?

The broader Millennial generation has observed the Baby Boomer orthodox Christian generation be staunchly conservative on morals and politics, while falling into moral scandals.

As a result, many Millennials have lost respect for the church because sometimes our values and actions have not been aligned with each other.

Interestingly, in key matters, Millennials most respect and want to emulate the Traditionalists rather than the Baby Boomers.

Celebrity culture

The church is not immune to celebrity culture. Just like any other industry, the church has its share of influencers. Social media has enabled a celebrity culture to develop around some worship leaders, pastors, and authors.

The macro-challenge

The church has been a laggard to change in culture and style. We are notoriously slow to adapt. We are at risk of becoming custodians of history and traditions, while the world and its cultures move on by.

Christianity is already in steep decline in Australia. Many other nations are following the same path.

It is estimated that Millennials will have 17 jobs across 5 careers in their lifetime. They will become used to rapid change in every area of their lives. The church will not escape this rate of change. Churches may find Millennials switching places of worship as many times as they change jobs.

What will happen to the local church if we do not adapt to these mega-trends? Will each church become another empty train carriage left to decay, or will we rally and refurbish the carriages to transport the Millennials?

What will happen to your church?

B

8 INNOVATIONS TO
LEADING MILLENNIALS

LEADING MILLENIALS

1 Use of Technology and Social Media

2 Relational Leadership Style

3 Collaborative Organizational Structure

4 Dynamic Program and Events

5 Depth in Spiritual Discipleship

6 Facilities That Represent Your Culture

7 Leadership in Finances

8 Emphasis on Social Rather than Political Engagement

INNOVATION 1
Use of Technology and Social Media

Millennials are the most technologically savvy generation.

They are genuine Digital Natives, immersed in a world of wearable devices, streaming music and videos, online communities, and social media. They have created much of the tech world. Millennials are designing virtual reality apps, engineering artificial intelligence, and redefining how humans work and play.

In the mind of the Millennial, any division between the offline and online worlds has become blurred, and perceived boundaries have become porous. There is no separation between what is online and offline, and vice versa. Both realities exist simultaneously.

This generation judges who we are offline by what they see online. They also assume that your online personality and branding match who you are offline.

Generational Trend: The convergence of online and offline

Every generation before the Millennials, however, makes a clear distinction between their offline and online world. To previous generations, offline and online worlds have little to do with each other.

Millennials are erasing the line between offline and online worlds.
BENJAMIN WINDLE

Typically, even someone from Generation X would consider having a coffee with a friend at a café as more real than online interaction. The real, tangible world and the building of community in physical spaces is valued as the higher of the two experiences between offline and online. Face-to-face contact ranks high because there is a distinction between the offline and online persona. Gen-Xers want to get to know the person beyond the assumed façade of technology. Put simply, older generations value their offline interactions more than their online ones, and they can draw a distinct line between the two.

This new generation of Millennials began erasing that line. Some Millennials and the majority of Gen Z have a paradigm of community, social interaction, and education that does not distinguish between offline and online. They are all one and the same: Millennials blend rather than bifurcate.

"When asking Generation Z (born 1995-2009) to describe what has defined and what has shaped their generation, the overwhelming response was technology. It is not only the number of devices and how frequently they interact with digital technologies, but how technology has shaped their thinking, facilitated communication, redefined community, become core to their learning, and become almost like a companion to them, which is extraordinary.

Connecting with others over social media platforms has become an ever more valid form of genuine socialisation, community building, and as a context for relationships to be formed, developed and maintained.

For Gen Z, communication is fluid and continual, with online communication seamlessly flowing on from any face-to-face interaction and vice versa—there is no real barrier or demarcation between online and offline. Social media is now so integrated into everyday life that it is no longer considered separate from other forms of interaction, and many find it easier to communicate online with their peers and social network than they do face-to-face. Not only is it considered a more 'real' and legitimate form of socialising than it is often given credit for by members of previous generations, the social interaction that occurs online is considered just as genuine and just as valid as if an interaction were occurring offline."

Hello Gen Z: Engaging the Generation of Post-Millennials

Racing cars, basketball, and the church

Le Mans is a prestigious 24-hour car race in France with 250,000 spectators. Its history is legendary, the stuff of innovation, efficiency, and endurance. Older Le Mans drivers train by strengthening their core muscles, building quick reflexes, and driving.

Not everyone, however, takes the same road to Le Mans. Recently, Nissan recruited a young gamer named Jann Mardenborough to drive their $12 million-plus car. At 23, Mardenborough had raced only on PlayStation. He acquired his F1 driving skills by practicing on simulated tracks.

For Mardenborough (and Nissan), there was no difference between an online and offline experience.

In 2018, the NBA, known for global basketball superstars Lebron James and Stephen Curry,

As churches lament and resist changes in technology, the NBA finds a way to monetize the use of video games and therefore create new opportunities and new revenue streams. Are sporting organisations more 'prophetic' and optimistic than Christian leaders and churches?

BENJAMIN WINDLE

started their fourth professional league. These basketball games aren't played on the hardwood of a basketball court—but rather on PlayStation. Players are drafted and signed to real teams that compete virtually. More than 1.6 million e-sports enthusiasts devote ten hours a week or more to the basketball league.

The new league—NBA2K video game league—shows the convergence of online and offline in this generation.

Simulated experiences are becoming the norm for Millennials as augmented/virtual reality changes the way people learn, train, and spend their leisure time.

As churches lament and resist changes in technology, the NBA finds a way to monetize the use of video games and therefore create new opportunities and new revenue streams. Are sporting organisations more 'prophetic' and optimistic than Christian leaders and churches?

We are reluctant to change and embrace technology, but it presents new opportunities. Technology unites, but only if it is embraced, rather than resisted.

The Challenge: Technology is a language not a tool

Millennials value connecting with others so much that they cannot envision giving up their communication tools. In fact, McCann Worldgroup discovered that half of Millennials would give up their sense of smell to keep their computer or mobile phone. They cannot fathom being without the ability to connect.

For Millennials, technology is a language for communication.

Remember that Millennials see no distinction between offline and online experiences. Technology helps them bridge that gap. Take away technology, and you take their most important communication platform.

Who you are online is perceived as who you are offline. The two are synonymous, not separate.

Practical Strategies and Approaches

The online community is not an 'add-on'—it is an authentic community

There are no on and off ramps on the Internet highway.

Millennials don't view an online community as an entry point to a real, offline community. The streams of online and offline communication converge into the same river, and conversations here are fluid.

The online community is as real to Millennials as the offline one. Our job is to extend our offline community to those online.

Invest in an authentic online expression

Millennials view people as a blend of offline reality and online presence. You cannot be one person when you're away from your computer or smartphone and another when you're back online.

Who you are online is perceived as who you are offline. The two are synonymous, not separate.

The quality of your website, podcast, social media accounts, online video, online content, and branding defines you. This is true for businesses and individuals as much as it is for churches. Ask yourself: how well does your online expression provide the same experience as your offline, traditional expression, and vice-versa?

Are we creating online community as intentionally as we do through Sundays, small groups, and offline options?

BENJAMIN WINDLE

Understanding the complete and fundamental convergence of offline and online has been my most significant personal discovery in unpacking innovations for leading Millennials and Gen Z. At the heart of it is the very nature of how Millennials see the world so differently regarding technology.

Technology is the new Sunday

Technology only moves forward. It's here to stay. Embrace new technology.

It offers amazing opportunities:

Communicate with people in new ways, such as via phone, email, and SMS.

Create community in new ways.

Disciple and pastor people in new ways to reach people where they are.

Create new educational pathways online to help people grow in Biblical knowledge.

Tell your story through social media

Telling our stories is one of the most important things we do. By sharing our narratives, we convey culture, articulate values, pass on learning, and inspire others.

To reach Millennials, you must tell the story of values, culture, and the why behind what you do.

Social media serves as a useful platform for this. However, there is a growing fatigue of how social media is being used. Sharing needs to be more sophisticated than posting 100 photos of our Sunday church services.

How we tell our stories should evolve.

"Don't use your social media to continually promote your business. That becomes annoying, and you'll get unfollowed pretty quickly."

Millennial Workforce: Cracking the Code to Generation Y in Your Company

Authenticity trumps excellence

The Millennial generation wants excellence—that is normal. But perfection is not the Millennial's goal, and that is the new normal.

With the advent of the Millennial generation came the concept of MVP, the Minimum Viable Product. While engineers designed and manufactured the most perfect product possible, the goal now is to produce the product or service that will minimally meet consumers' needs and solve their problems. The process is quick, efficient, but not final.

Any future MVP iterations are the result of consumer feedback.

Mostly, Millennials want authenticity, and they honor vulnerability in a leader and preacher.

Millennials don't want a 'cool church' where modern production is a thin veneer plastered over an old Boomer culture. They want something they can relate to.

"For young people today, relational warmth is the new cool."

Growing Young: Six Essential Strategies to Help Young People Discover and Love Your Church

Millennials don't want a 'cool church' where modern production is a thin veneer plastered over an old Boomer culture. They want something they can relate to.

BENJAMIN WINDLE

TWEET THIS

INNOVATION 2
Relational Leadership Style

For Millennials, leadership is not about power.

Once again, Millennials are fundamentally changing the way we understand leadership.

Generational Trend: Millennials follow relationship not authority

Millennials no longer respond to power and authority in and of itself. The days of "because I said so" and "do as I say, not as I do" are vanishing.

Authoritative power does not connect with Millennials—relationship does.

> "Power is decaying. To put it simply, power no longer buys as much as it did in the past."
>
> The End of Power: From Boardrooms to Battlefields and Churches to States, Why Being in Charge Isn't What it Used to Be

The Challenge: A theology of spiritual authority should not become an authoritarian leadership style

In his book, The 5 Levels of Leadership, John Maxwell relegates position/authority to the lowest level of leadership. Sometimes, in our theology of being the Senior Pastor, Leader, or Elder, our style gets stuck in this mode.

In the Boomer generation, leading from authority may not have been great leadership, but the hierarchy in organizations was an accepted norm. Today, not only is authoritative leadership ineffective—it is fatal to a culture.

5. Pinnacle
Respect
People follow because of who you are & what you represent.

4. People Development
Reproduction
People follow because of what you have done for them.

3. Production
Results
People follow because of what you have done for the organisation.

2. Permission
Relationships
People follow you because they want to.

1. Position
Rights
People follow you because they have to.

MILLENNIALS RESIST MOST
TRADITIONAL STRUCTURES
BECAUSE THEY WERE RAISED IN
A LEARNING ENVIRONMENT THAT
EMBRACED COLLABORATION.

BENJAMIN WINDLE

Practical Strategies and Approaches

Lead from authority but not with authority

Millennial leadership style is relational and strategic.

Leadership requires both skill and strategy, but Millennial leadership is about creating connections with people. The saying "people don't care how much you know until they know how much you care" is truer today than it ever has been before.

Leaders must first work on the relationship and then apply strategy.

The death of authority

Ask yourself this key question: how would I lead if I had no organizational authority?

If you consider that your people didn't have to do what you said, you would have to rely more on relationship and communication.

Relational

Millennials respond to the relational leader.

> "It would be easy for us to dismiss very talented people (who would bring value to our organizations) as being unmanageable or disrespectful of authority. We need to understand that, in their minds, they're just trying to learn and fully understand concepts."
>
> **Millennial Workforce: Cracking the Code to Generation Y in Your Company**

Leading Millennials is more about being the guide on the side, not a sage on a stage. It's about sitting next to rather than in front of.

INNOVATION 3
Collaborative Organizational Structure

Many organizational structures in the past have been built like a ladder. Decisions seem to rest with people at the top of the organization, while others at the lower rungs serve to implement these decisions.

Generational Trend: Millennials are team-oriented and collaborative, and resist structure

Lead pastor and college professor Dr. Frank Damazio summarized this trend: "Millennials are mercurial, and Boomers are linear; Millennials are fluid."

> "Millennials want the opportunity to be innovative and collaborate together. They grew up going to school with constant group projects.
>
> A team-oriented and collaborative work environment is critical for Millennials in the workplace."
>
> Look at Google and Facebook and see how their offices are laid out, the way they have break rooms, and how everybody works together. This is a break from the hierarchy culture that has existed in big business for decades. Millennials want access to top management."
>
> Millennial Workforce: Cracking the Code to Generation Y in Your Company

Millennials resist most traditional structures because they were raised in a learning environment that embraced collaboration.

Millennials can grow your church if you'll listen to their ideas.
BENJAMIN WINDLE

The Challenge: Help churches evolve from a hierarchal organization of ladders to circles of collaboration

Ladders represent command and control, top-down organizations that dictate to subordinates.

Those at the entry level of organizations, the lowest ladder rungs, are often given seemingly meaningless tasks to do, with little or no input in the process of how these could be most effectively done or changed. As a result, disengagement and disillusionment become the norm.

In the minds of Millennials, the ladder style of organizational management leaves much to be desired.

By contrast, circle-style organization shows teams within teams, with defined leadership but also specific outcomes.

Practical Strategies and Approaches

Become a listening organization

Listening is the best way to reach Millennials who want to be involved and be heard.

Have a conversation with Millennials, and you'll discover that they want to devote themselves to a cause. They want to work from a place of significance, where they can be relevant and leave an impact on their world.

That's where you come in.

To reach Millennials, you have to hire them—but hiring a few Millennials won't solve the problem. We must platform Millennials to reach Millennials—and yet, putting more young people on the stage is not the only solution.

Reaching Millennials must go deeper than surface level. Go deep by creating a structure that respects diverse opinions, rewards collaboration, and encourages fluid work processes.

Create an environment of training and mentoring

Millennials are hungry: they want to learn.

In a PwC's report, Millennials at work, two of the top three factors that make an organization an attractive employer were 'opportunities for career progression' and 'excellent training/development programs.'

Make it a habit to deliberately disrespect your own organizational chart and instead communicate at a grassroots level.

BENJAMIN WINDLE

"Millennials are on the path to becoming the most educated generation in America's history. The Millennials understand the power behind a mentor. That is why we want one. Three out of four Millennials would like a leader to come beside them and teach them leadership skills.

Indeed, another moniker that might fit the Millennials is "the learning generation." When we asked them to respond to the statement, "I have a great appetite for learning," the results were impressive. An overwhelming 95 percent of the Millennials answered the question positively."

The Millennials

Define the difference between Management vs. Leadership

Think for a moment about the people in your organization. Do they work for you or follow you?

Millennials want to follow you. They want you to lead them, not manage them, because they are eager to build strong relationships.

Consider this:

Management = systems

Leadership = relationships

Don't *lead* through systems. Systems are about processes, not people.

Don't *manage* through relationships. Relationships are about people, not processes.

> "Leadership is about relating, listening, collaborating and empowering, not about commanding or demanding."
>
> Hello Gen Z: Engaging the Generation of Post-Millennials

The most successful leaders merge management skills with leadership skills. They rely on their management skills for taking care of the day-to-day operations, but they use their leadership skills to take care of the people in the organization.

Skip level communication

Organizational charts are helpful for management, but they don't have to dictate how a leader relates or communicates.

If you require that all communication travels through tightly structured conduits that push information bites up and down the ladder, you're missing out on one of the greatest strengths Millennials bring with them: their ability to generate ideas that are productive and useful to the organization.

Make it a habit to deliberately disrespect your organizational chart: instead, communicate at a grassroots level.

INNOVATION 4

Dynamic Program and Events

Generational Trend: Millennials are time-poor and need to see value

Today's demands of a 24/7 world keep Millennials busier than any other generation before them. Texts, emails, and phone calls pour into their inboxes as they tend to their jobs, children, and homes. Scheduling conflicts force prioritization.

With so little time to go around, Millennials want to know that the time they do invest in an activity is worthwhile.

The Challenge: Church calendars, programs, and schedules need to be reinvented for a new world

This is highly specific for every context. A great starting point is to look at every event, program, and meeting on the church calendar and ask questions such as, "Why do we do it this way? Is this still the best way? Is this timeslot best for our volunteers and staff, or best to reach unchurched Millennials?" Eliminate programs that are no longer fruitful. Streamline your weekly events. And the things you do – do them well. Consolidation enables you to put more focus, strategy, and quality into the meetings and events you do.

Practical Strategies and Approaches

Make weekly Sunday attendance a unique value proposition

Today's church-goers have plenty of ways to attend services without ever stepping foot inside your building. Passive worship opportunities have existed for a long time in the form of radio, television, podcasts, and live-streaming video. More interactive involvement now includes virtual reality worship.

What do Millennials get from attending a Sunday church service that they can't get online?

Stay in 'beta' mode

The only way an organization can remain lean enough to survive is by regularly reviewing what's working, what's not working, and what needs changing.

"In the tech industry, the term for this stage of development is "beta"—never fully baked, always in flux, focused yet open to change."

Betaball: How Silicon Valley and Science Built One of the Greatest Basketball Teams in History

In addressing the question of spiritual discipleship in Millennials, the temptation is to find quick-fixes and address surface-level issues.

We have to go deeper, because the eternal values of spiritual discipleship are more important than ever.

Discipleship is not about growing a big church. It's about growing big people.

DISCIPLESHIP IS NOT ABOUT GROWING A BIG CHURCH. IT'S ABOUT GROWING BIG PEOPLE.

BENJAMIN WINDLE

INNOVATION 5

Depth in Spiritual Discipleship

Generational Trend: Millennials are biblically illiterate, but passionate about learning

Millennials may not come with vast knowledge of the Bible. Even basic Bible stories have fallen out of their common culture and experience. This generation is passionate about acquiring new knowledge, and it has an insatiable desire to learn by exploring meaning in depth, rather than skimming the surface for superficial understanding.

The Challenge: There is a crucial need to build depth in a shallow culture

The present generational trends offer a unique opportunity for anyone seeking to teach and guide those looking for meaning in their lives. It's vital that the church steps up to meet this opportunity to reach Millennials where they are. Millennials yearn for substance and meaning in their lives, but they often don't know where to find it. As a result, they seek out and engage in shallow experiences that leave them feeling emptier than when they started.

> "A keenly felt emptiness, resulting from a secularized, materialistic world, has led to a hunger for something more, but many are unable to go further than the search for an experience."
>
> **Meet Generation Z: Understanding and Reaching the New Post-Christian World**

We need to go deep.

Practical Strategies and Approaches

Teach leaders the heart and practice of being a shepherd, not being a star

You've heard of servant leadership, the kind where leaders serve others rather than themselves. Shepherds serve, too. They serve their flocks. Leaders focus on the message and those receiving it, not the messenger.

Everything to do with pastoring comes out of the Shepherd's heart. The Shepherd exists for the sheep; the sheep don't exist for the Shepherd.

To be an effective leader, a shepherd of the flock, you have to be a sheep yourself, even smelling like sheep. Don't resent the sheep, or withdraw from the sheep, or have a few favorite sheep.

Go deeper with discipleship

Today's prevailing culture is image-driven. This culture has neglected its inner voice, and although they may not realize it, they want help.

> **A key phrase I use to teach leaders is this: you don't need to be famous, you just need to be faithful.**
> **BENJAMIN WINDLE**

What you use for attraction, you must continue with for retention.

If you use gimmicks, fads, or hype—you better keep that up every week. If you build the story of your church on being the it church, the cool church, or the image church, be warned that you can't be those things forever. Fads fade away, and trends evolve. In a superficial culture, depth is attractive.

Provide Bible teaching and basic doctrine

It may seem overly simplistic, but to lead a generation with no biblical background or common knowledge, the church must assume just that: that there exists a fundamental need to provide Bible teaching and basic doctrine.

We must lay the foundation.

IN A SUPERFICIAL CULTURE, DEPTH IS ATTRACTIVE.

BENJAMIN WINDLE

Provide content-driven courses and lessons to help them learn

On top of this foundation—basic Bible teaching and doctrine—provide content-driven courses and experiences to help Millennials learn and understand their place in life. With an attitude of questioning and an appetite to learn, Millennials and Gen Z can find answers to their questions within the church.

With its content-driven courses and lessons, the church can provide something concrete and solid in a fluid, shifting world.

I walk into a room and resonate with a culture. A culture is the sum total of all the tangibles and intangibles—how people dress, what signage catches the eye, the brand of coffee machine, the volume of music, the age of door-greeters, and the printed materials. It's also whether you use commercial or ambient lighting, orderly rows or casual seating, and how the acoustics contribute to conversation or choke it.

INNOVATION 6

Facilities That Represent Your Culture

Generational Trend: For Millennials, physical design communicates culture

Millennials read the language of physical space as a communication of culture.

The Challenge: Church facilities cannot be simply functional – they must be culturally experiential

How do your buildings and the physical environment actively facilitate community?

Do the spaces communicate consideration for the way people physically interact—particularly those who find personal interaction more daunting than its virtual counterpart?

Practical Strategies and Approaches

Provide what technology cannot

Millennials can get the best preaching and worship from around the world on their phone.

How can you compete with technology like that? By providing people with things that technology cannot offer.

> "They have a longing for real authentic offline relationships but can lack skills in knowing how to foster them."
>
> Hello Gen Z: Engaging the Generation of Post-Millennials

Create a physical experience that facilitates community

A great case study is the dramatic, strategic change in shopping malls.

In the malls of ten years ago, the quality, people flow, design, and end-outcome was different. Food courts were places of cheap, take-away food that was fast but hardly nutritious. At the time, however, people preferred shopping in large department stores, where they could try on clothing and check the quality of merchandise in person.

Technology has disrupted this industry. Nowadays, people can often buy a product cheaper on Amazon, for example.

People who shop online find that there's no traffic, no trying to find a parking place (or remembering where you left your car), and no wandering through the mall to find what you're looking for.

The church needs to reconsider how it teaches about finances and promotes fiduciary responsibility and discipline in a financial age of overwhelming consumerism.

Pacific Fair, Gold Coast Before and After a $580M Renovation

And so, today's shopping centers have recognized the need to offer something unique. Shopping design involves large gathering areas, sitting areas, restaurants, high-end gourmet food eateries, deli/market style grocery stores, entertainment, and live music.

To attract consumers back to a physical space, they have created an experience that cannot be replicated online. Shopping in person once again makes coming together worthwhile!

As our online and offline images converge—prompting us to rethink how our online expression reflects our real or physical culture—the same focus on intentionality applies to the offline.

Think about facility areas such as foyers, café spaces, and gathering points that can help foster connection and community. See these areas as equally important as the main worship auditorium.

Invest in coffee

A coffee represents much more than a beverage. The kind of beans, brand of machine, cups, and physical café-style spaces communicate a message of culture.

Coffee culture should be an investment. Good coffee communicates a heart of hospitality and genuine care.

Consider how long people stay on average after a worship service. If they run out the door and empty the parking lot faster than you can wave goodbye, something's not right. If, however, they stay for fellowship after the service, your investment in developing relationships is working. Community and an offline experience will become more important – how are our facilities reflecting this?

Your church culture tells a story—the story of who you are. Culture is an investment. Is there a need in your story for a little coffee culture?

Community and an offline experience will become more important - how are our facilities reflecting this?

BENJAMIN WINDLE

INNOVATION 7
Leadership in Finances

Generational Trend: Millennials are the most consumeristic generation in history

This generation engages in robust spending. As a result, Millennials have tremendous purchasing power. Over the course of their lifetimes, they will spend more than $10 trillion.

The Millennial generation was born into a consumeristic society, then schooled in it. Now they live in it every day. Consumerism is a major narrative of their lives.

The Challenge: Traditionalists and Boomers are key donors, with Millennials giving less to the church

Financial support of the church has been left mainly to Traditionalist and Boomers, who tithed their 10% and sometimes provided additional gifts in the form of bequests.

It's what they did, and they did it without question.

Millennials, on the other hand, have been less likely to tithe and more likely to question.

So, how do we understand their hesitation to commit to tithing and bridge the gap?

Practical Strategies and Approaches

Keep the greater cause of giving in front of Millennials
Millennials are most attracted to causes. The dominant narrative about finances should be stewardship and a financial worldview.

Millennials need to be taught a Christian financial worldview
The act of giving can't simply be 'just give'—it has to be, 'Here's how to live in an age of consumerism, and here is why giving helps you do that. Here is where tithing helps you do that.'

The Millennial generation wants to see where and how their money will make a difference in bringing about unity.

The act of giving can't simply be 'just give'—it has to be, 'Here's how to live in an age of consumerism, and here is why giving helps you do that. Here is where tithing helps you do that.'

BENJAMIN WINDLE

Consistently teach on biblical tithing, stewardship, and Kingdom Finance

For more resources on this subject, please go to www.benjaminwindle.com to discover more.

Invest in children's ministry

What's the most important ministry to reach Millennials? Children's ministry.

Young families are child-centric. They will go to places that their kids enjoy.

"Here's the lesson: you can drop the ball in the service but ace it with the kids and still have a chance that a family will return. But no matter how good the service is, if the children's ministry is bad, the family won't come back."

Meet Generation Z: Understanding and Reaching the New Post-Christian World

INNOVATION 8
Emphasis on Social Rather Than Political Engagement

Generational trend: Millennials are turned off by pastors in politics

The challenge: Balancing social change with a politically skeptical generation

Instead of making political statements—focus on the justice issues behind policies

Millennials are highly socially conscious.

Instead of making specific political statements, consider focusing on justice issues, like feeding the poor, eradicating sex trafficking, helping orphans, helping those in poverty, etc.

These social issues attract Millennials because they see the efforts behind them as including people rather than excluding them. For example, during the Australian plebiscite of 2017, the church treated Same Sex Marriage as a theological issue, but Millennials saw it as a civil rights movement. Millennials are very politically diverse.

Practical strategies and approaches

Use language that they use

Dieu vous aime et a envoyé son fils.

Did that first line make sense? Probably not, unless you speak French! Before I translate it, let me tell you a story.

One summer, I went to France with my wife for a vacation. It was breathtaking to see some of the old church buildings in Paris. One Sunday, we decided to visit one. However, neither my wife nor I spoke French. The only word I understood from the preacher was "bonjour." We experienced a cultural barrier. Sure, the building was magnificent and the people seemed friendly, but the preaching was in a different language. We couldn't understand it, and therefore, apart from some nice tourist photos, we found the church unhelpful to our lives.

Back to the earlier line: translated to English, it reads, "God loves you and sent his Son."

One need not travel to France to experience the dilemma of cultural barriers in church. We face it every day in our journey of being the church in a secular culture. I use the opening line and the story of visiting France to illustrate that if the church does not communicate in a relevant way, then it is not useful to people's lives. The message may be sent, but the message must also be received. One of the challenges we face is to speak the language of the people and culture we are reaching.

To attract and retain Millennials, avoid words and descriptions that exclude individuals or groups of people. Keep in mind that Millennials even despise the moniker used to describe their generation because it separates them from other generations.

Millennials are the future. And the future is now.

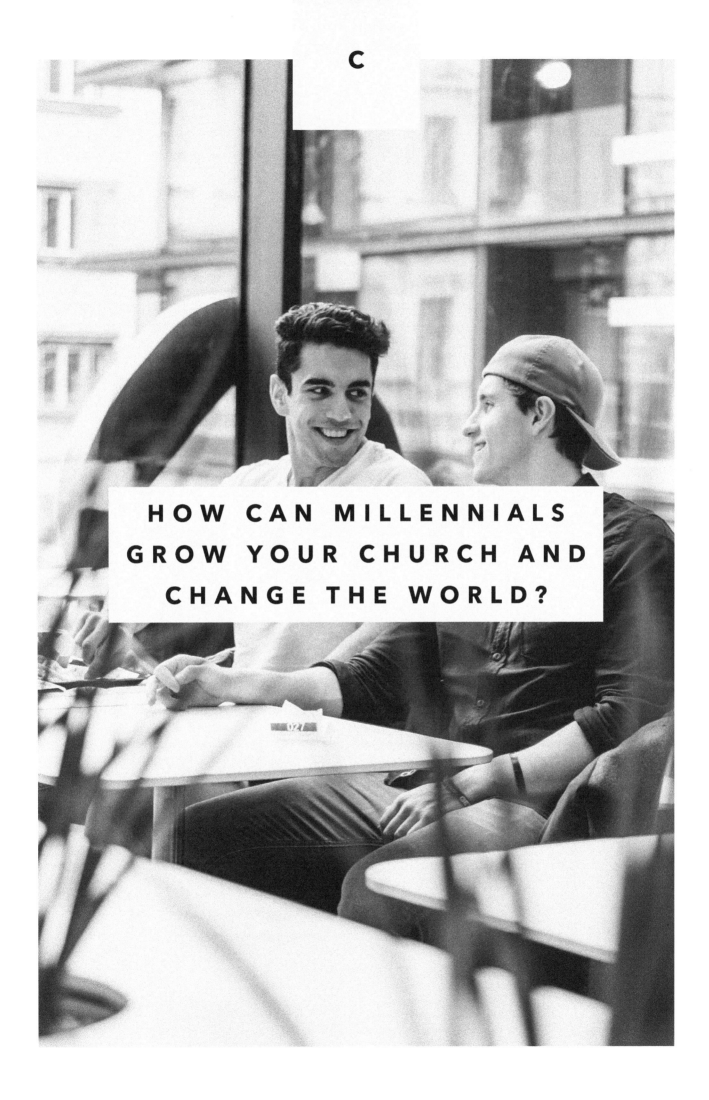

C

HOW CAN MILLENNIALS
GROW YOUR CHURCH AND
CHANGE THE WORLD?

Pausing to consider how we lead and reach Millennials provides a significant and positive opportunity to rethink multi-generation church leadership.

The Millennial generation represents the most significant shift the Western church has experienced in recent years. We are facing a mega-shift in culture, church attendance, religious beliefs, and how to merge guiding principles with daily life.

Millennials bring new ideas and question the status quo, but importantly, see optimism in their futures. They will give their hearts and lives to a cause if they are respected and invited to understand its significance and impact.

By effectively reaching and leading Millennials, you have the power to grow your church for future generations, if you can harness their thirst for knowledge and the belief that they can do something significant.

It is my prayer that this will guide and inspire you.

The local church is a spiritual home for the city. It is God's plan on earth. It is a family of God's people. It is a city within a city. It is a light on a hill. It is God's House!

Micah 4:1-2 tells us that the church will not decline as society progresses. Rather, as history moves towards its last chapter before the return of Jesus, the church will rise in prominence! "In the last days, the mountain of the Lord's house will be the highest of all— the most important place on earth. It will be raised above the other hills, and people from all over the world will stream there to worship. People from many nations will come and say, "Come, let us go up to the mountain of the Lord, to the house of Jacob's God. There he will teach us his ways, and we will walk in his paths."

By effectively reaching and leading Millennials, you have the power to grow your church for future generations, if you can harness their thirst for knowledge and the belief that they can do something significant.

BENJAMIN WINDLE

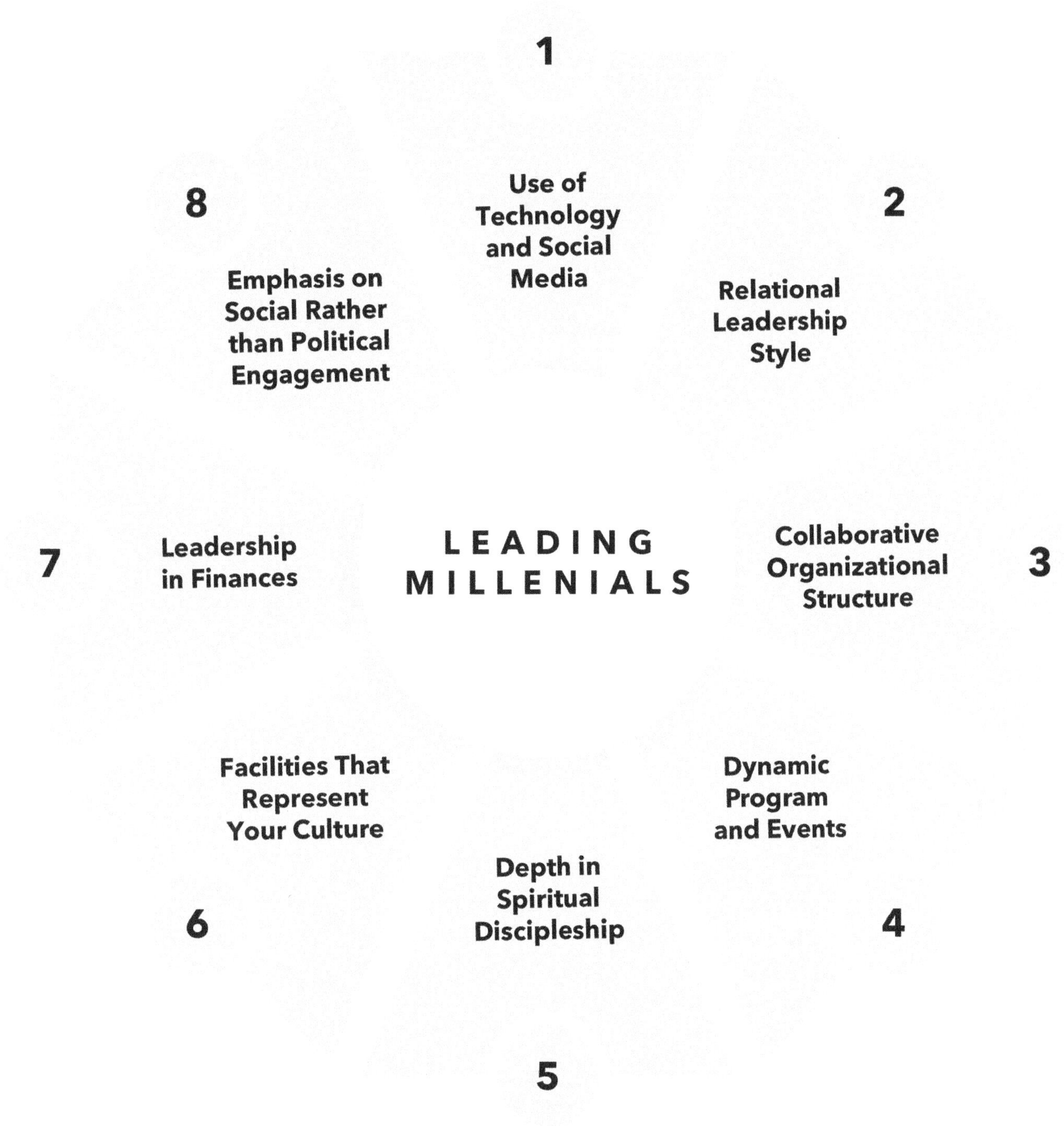

1

**Use of
Technology
and Social
Media**

8

**Emphasis on
Social Rather
than Political
Engagement**

2

**Relational
Leadership
Style**

7

**Leadership
in Finances**

LEADING
MILLENIALS

**Collaborative
Organizational
Structure**

3

**Facilities That
Represent
Your Culture**

**Dynamic
Program
and Events**

6

**Depth in
Spiritual
Discipleship**

4

5

D

SCRIPTURES ON GENERATIONS

God's plan for his people has always been generational. God counts in generations, moves through generations, and blesses through generations.

4 One generation passes away, and another generation comes; But the earth abides forever.

ECCLESIASTES 1:4 (NKJV)

2 …for I will speak to you in a parable. I will teach you hidden lessons from our past— 3stories we have heard and known, stories our ancestors handed down to us.

4 We will not hide these truths from our children; we will tell the next generation about the glorious deeds of the LORD, about his power and his mighty wonders.

5 For he issued his laws to Jacob; he gave his instructions to Israel. He commanded our ancestors to teach them to their children,

6 so the next generation might know them— even the children not yet born— and they in turn will teach their own children.

7 So each generation should set its hope anew on God, not forgetting his glorious miracles and obeying his commands.

PSALM 78:2-7 (NLT)

7 "I will confirm my covenant with you and your descendants after you, from generation to generation. This is the everlasting covenant: I will always be your God and the God of your descendants after you.

GENESIS 17:7 (NLT)

50 He shows mercy from generation to generation to all who fear him.

LUKE 1:50 (NLT)

17 All those listed above include fourteen generations from Abraham to David, fourteen from David to the Babylonian exile, and fourteen from the Babylonian exile to the Messiah.

MATTHEW 1:17 (NLT)

10 After that generation died, another generation grew up who did not acknowledge the LORD or remember the mighty things he had done for Israel.

JUDGES 2:10 (NLT)

6 so the next generation might know them— even the children not yet born— and they in turn will teach their own children.

PSALM 78:6 (NLT)

8 I will bring you into the land I swore to give to Abraham, Isaac, and Jacob. I will give it to you as your very own possession. I am the LORD!

EXODUS 6:8 (NLT)

SO EACH GENERATION SHOULD SET ITS HOPE ANEW ON GOD, NOT FORGETTING HIS GLORIOUS MIRACLES & OBEYING HIS COMMANDS

PSALM 78:2-7 (NLT)

E

SUGGESTED READING

Meet Generation Z: Understanding and Reaching the New Post-Christian World
2017, BY JAMES EMERY WHITE

Hello Gen Z: Engaging the Generation of Post-Millennials
2017, BY CLAIRE MADDEN

The Millennials: Connecting to America's Largest Generation
2011, BY THOM S. RAINER AND JESS RAINER

Growing Young: Six Essential Strategies to Help Young People Discover and Love Your Church
2016, BY KARA POWELL, JAKE MULDER, AND BRAD GRIFFIN

A Generation of Sociopaths: How the Baby Boomers Betrayed America
2017, BY BRUCE CANNON GIBNEY

Millennial Workforce: Cracking the Code to Generation Y in Your Company
2017, BY JAVIER MONTES

Kids These Days: Human Capital and the Making of Millennials
2017, BY MALCOLM HARRIS

Generational IQ: Christianity Isn't Dying, Millennials Aren't the Problem, and the Future is Bright
2015, BY HAYDN SHAW AND GINGER KOLBABA

The Greatest Generation
1998, BY TOM BROKAW

The End of Power: From Boardrooms to Battlefields and Churches to States, Why Being in Charge Isn't What It Used to Be
2013, BY MOISES NAIM

References

i https://religionnews.com/2018/06/26/why-millennials-are-really-leaving-religion-its-not-just-politics-folks/

ii https://www.prri.org/research/prri-rns-poll-nones-atheist-leaving-religion/

iii https://influencemagazine.com/Practice/Five-Reasons-Millennials-Are-Leaving-the-Church

iv https://faithit.com/12-reasons-millennials-over-church-sam-eaton/

v https://edition.cnn.com/2015/05/12/living/pew-religion-study/index.html

vi https://www1.cbn.com/cbnnews/us/2019/january/an-epidemic-why-millennials-are-abandoning-the-church

New Book by Benjamin Windle

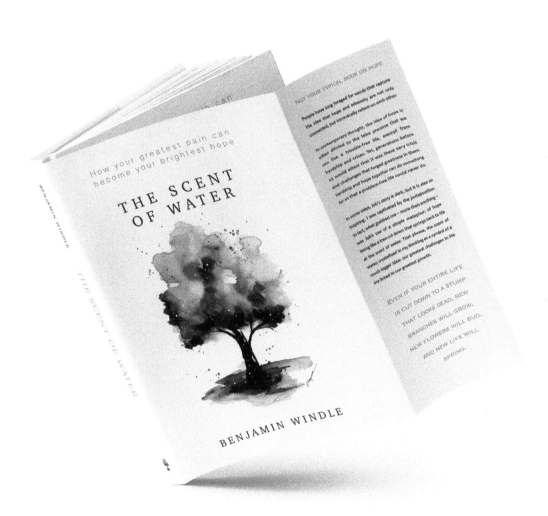

Go to www.thescentofwaterbook.com to get a free chapter and advance information on the upcoming release.

Not your typical book on hope.

People have long foraged for words that capture the idea that hope and adversity are not only connected, but intrinsically reliant on each other.

In contemporary thought, the idea of hope is often diluted to the false promise that we can live a trouble-free life, exempt from hardship and crises. Yet, generations before us would attest that it was these very trials and challenges that forged greatness in them. Hardship and hope together can do something for us that a problem-free life could never do.

...

In some ways, Job's story is dark, but it is also so inspiring. I was captivated by the juxtaposition. In fact, what grabbed me – more than anything – was Job's use of a simple metaphor: of hope being like a tree cut down that springs back to life at the scent of water. That phrase, the scent of water, crystallized in my thinking as a symbol of a much bigger idea: our greatest challenges in life are linked to our greatest growth.

Even if your entire life is cut down to a stump that looks dead, new branches will grow, new flowers will bud, and new life will spring.

In this unique and compelling book, you will discover the secret to weathering the storms of life, learn how to rise above daily imperfections, recognize where to turn in the midst of pain, know how to survive crises and come out better, understand how to filter worry and stress, and gain an ultimate perspective on every challenge you face in life.

You can end the quest for a trouble-free life, and harness every adversity to your advantage."

Get an advance free chapter now at www.thescentofwaterbook.com

Download and share a copy at
www.millennialswhitepaper.com

www.benjaminwindle.com
contact@benjaminwindle.com

thrive co